RADSPORTS GUIDES

WAKEBOARDING

TRACY NELSON MAURER

Rourke
Publishing LLC
Vero Beach, Florida 32964

www.rourkepublishing.com

Project Assistance
David Williams, Editor/Writer/Rider for WakeWorld.com Online Wakeboarding Magazine.

Also, the author extends appreciation to Fox Racing, Dallas Friday, Shaun Murray, Mike Maurer, and Kendall and Lois M. Nelson.

Photo Credits: Cover, pages 7 & 8: © Corbis Images; pages 11, 12, 16, 20, 21, 24, 25, 27, 28, 33, 34: © CSL; pages 4, 37 & 38: © Stanley Chou/Getty Images; page 38: © jamie Squire/Allsport

Cover photo: Wakeboarders practice a lot to learn awesome tricks like this.

Editor: Frank Sloan

Cover and page design: Nicola Stratford

Notice: This book contains information that is true, complete and accurate to the best of our knowledge. However, the author and Rourke Publishing LLC offer all recommendations and suggestions without any guarantees and disclaim all liability incurred in connection with the use of this information.

Safety first! Activities appearing or described in this publication may be dangerous. Always wear safety gear. Even with complete safety gear, risk of injury still exists.

Library of Congress Cataloging-in-Publication Data

Maurer, Tracy, 1965-
  Wakeboarding / Tracy Nelson Maurer.
      p. cm. — (Radsports guides)
Summary: Surveys the history, equipment, techniques, and safety factors of wakeboarding, a sport in which a rider is pulled behind a motorboat standing on a board that resembles a short surfboard.
Includes bibliographical references and index.
  ISBN 1-58952-281-8 (hard)
  1. Wakeboarding—Juvenile literature. [1. Wakeboarding.] I. Title. Wakeboarding. II. Title.
  GV840.W34 M29 2002
  797.3'2—dc21
                                                    2002008228

Printed in the USA

CG/CG

TABLE OF CONTENTS

Riders use wakes as ramps for big-air tricks.

SPORTS ASSORTMENT

Surfing, skateboarding, snowboarding, and waterskiing each deliver awesome moves. Wakeboarding takes a bit from each of these sports for a totally different "extreme" experience.

A wakeboard looks like a thick snowboard or a short surfboard. Boot-like bindings on the board give the rider a snowboard-style stance, or body position. A motorboat pulls the wakeboarder by a long rope. The boat driver tries to deliver big wakes for the rider to use as ramps for big-air tricks.

chapter

ONE

Yappers thought that wakeboarding was a fad. They thought surfing, skateboarding, snowboarding, and waterskiing were fads, too. (Sense a trend here?)

SKURFING? SKIBOARDING?

Before 1985, surfers held onto ropes from boats to amp up their fun. Then surfer Tony Finn screwed foot straps onto a short surfboard for more control and more tricks. He called his new ride a skurfer. At about the same time, Jimmy Redmon added foot straps to his surfboard-style waterski. He called his ride a skiboard.

Skiboards and skurfers caught the attention of waterski manufacturer Herb O'Brien. He used **compression molding** to make a strong, lightweight board. His **neutrally buoyant** design meant it didn't bob in deep water. Riders could hold it underwater to start up easier than on a skurfer.

O'Brien's thin edge also allowed riders to carve turns. His board's wide shape added stability. Phasers, or dimples on the bottom, broke water away from the board so it planed smoothly, too. Other manufacturers followed. Redmon created the first non-directional, "twin-tip" shape—matching curves and fins at the tip and tail.

A WORLDWIDE SPORT SENSATION

The sport became official in 1992. O'Brien's team called it "wakeboarding," because riders could jump off wakes. The team also wanted the world to know wakeboarding was a completely new sport, easier to learn than skiing. The name stuck.

By 2000, wakeboarding counted some three million riders worldwide. It's still gaining fans—fast. Thanks to O'Brien, Redmon, and others, you don't have to be Hercules to wrestle yourself a ride. Nearly anyone, at any age, can wakeboard!

Wakeboards use fins at the tip and the tail for action in both directions!

The proper stance makes learning tricks easier.

PRE-SPLASH ZONE

Before you hop on a board, know how to swim. No excuses. Then buy a lifejacket or ski vest, called a **personal flotation device** (PFD), approved by the U.S. Coast Guard. All boaters and wakeboarders should wear PFDs. Check the label to see if the PFD holds your weight.

Try your PFD in shallow water. Does your head stay above water? Don't use it if the straps and fabric are worn or torn. After a session, hang the PFD to dry. Storing a wet PFD rots the fabric. It adds a rank odor, too.

STOMP A STANCE

Before you buy a board and bindings, know your stance. A wakeboarder stands sideways on the board with his or her toes pointed to one edge. But which edge?

On land, stand with your feet together and ask a buddy to sneak up behind you and shove you. (Most brothers and sisters will gladly help with this experiment, too.) Which foot do you use to steady yourself? Put the same foot forward on your wakeboard.

Left foot forward? You're a regular foot. Right foot forward? You're a goofy foot. Skateboarders, surfers, and snowboarders usually plant the same foot forward on a wakeboard.

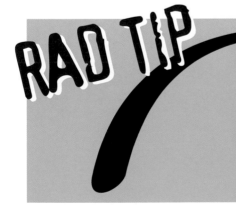

Rent-a-Rides
If your buddy's stance is the same as yours, ask to borrow his board before you buy one of your own. Some shops rent or demo (demonstrate) wakeboards, too.

FIND THE RIGHT RIDE

Cool graphics blaze across the deck and bottoms of wakeboards. Don't let the scenery fool you. Read the buyers' guides. Ask around. Does it pop off the wake? How well does it carve? Can it handle spins in the air and on the water?

Boards weigh about 6 or 7 pounds (2.72 or 3.17 kg) or less. At different times, manufacturers have tried foam core, carbon fiber, aluminum honeycomb, balsa wood, or other materials to lighten the boards. Grommets, or smaller kids, usually look for 15-inch (38-cm) width. Everyone else rides boards between 16 and 18 inches (40.6 and 45.7 cm) wide.

Tips and tails curve in, curve out, double-dip, and more. Rails, or edges, also bump up high or barely blip the deck surface.

The rave board this season may be forgotten next season. Test ride it before you spend about $100 to $700 on the board. Pay for performance, not just the looks.

THE OUTS AND INS OF FINS

Some boards come with molded-in fins. Others use removable fins. Some have one fin at each end. Some use several fins. Boarders sometimes use sandpaper to shape the fin just where it butts the board. This keeps air pockets from gagging the board's flow.

Rocker, or the upward curve at the tip and tail, also varies from board to board. More rocker adds pop, but cuts speed.

Don't let the graphics fool you! Find the right board for your skills and size.

A wet binding will help your foot slip into your binding.

TIES THAT BIND

Bindings hold your ankles and feet in place with ties, buckles, hook-and-loop straps, or other clever systems. Special designs help water flow through the boots. Prices range from $100 to $400.

Find the right size and take time to adjust the fit. Your bindings should feel snug, but not so tight that your toes turn blue or feel numb. Bindings loosen up after serious session time. You want the bindings to stay on when you biff—unless it's a major crash. Then you want them to release before you wreck your knee, leg, or ankle.

SLIP AND SLIDE IN

Dip your boots under water before you try to squish into them. Use binding lubes sold in your local board shop to help your feet slide in. They work.

Dish soap or baby shampoo that is **water-soluble** and **biodegradable**, also works, but might dry out your bindings over time.

Don't use baby oil, petroleum jelly, or other oil lubes. They don't break down in water, but they break down the material in your bindings. Oils also harm critters in the water.

ADJUST YOUR ANGLE

Bindings feel odd enough without placing them in the wrong position. Most **newbies** start with the back foot pointed straight across the board or a bit toward the nose. The front foot angles more toward the nose, but not straight at the tip. Newbies also ride further back on the board so they can control the tail fin better.

When your skills advance, try centering your bindings. Both feet might be straight across, or **perpendicular** to, the board. Some riders like them slightly "ducked" out, with the big toes angled away from each other. Put the bindings where you feel the most control riding **revert**, throwing surface tricks, and landing **aerials**.

Newbie Straps

Newbies wipe out. A lot. Instead of dawging around with bindings, you might try bungie or sandal straps to hold your feet. They release quickly in a crash. They're also easy to put on. You lose ankle support without boots, so watch your stance! Are they as safe as boot bindings? Depends who you ask.

TWO TO TOW

Unlike other extreme sports, wakeboarding requires two other people besides the rider for each session. Find a boat driver and a spotter. The spotter watches your hand signals and tells the driver what to do. The spotter also lets the driver know when the rider falls down.

Talk to the driver about speed. Depending on the rider's size, newbies start between 16 and 20 miles (25.7 and 32.2 km) per hour. Most riders never go faster than 24 miles (38.6 km) per hour because the boat's wake flattens out then. Once you feel comfortable on your board, try different speeds to find the best one for you and your boat.

chapter TWO

A large rear-view mirror helps the boat driver to keep an eye on the wakeboarder at all times.

BOAT SAFETY

The standard safety rules for boating apply to wakeboard boats. Your driver should complete an approved safety course. It's the law in some states. Take the course, too. Knowing more about boating makes you better at wakeboarding.

Towing a wakeboarder looks easy. It's not. The driver must keep a steady speed. If the rider slows the boat on a big carve, the driver lightly amps the throttle for a smooth pull. Or, if the rider catches air, the driver might back off the gas slightly. Drivers avoid big steering changes.

When the rider biffs, the driver quickly drops to neutral. Then the driver turns the boat slowly and idles back to the rider. Ripping a U-turn plows up big rollers that chop the smooth water, making riding more difficult once the rider gets back up.

SIGNAL CODES

Yelling to the driver doesn't work. Wind and engine noise drown your words. Make sure you and the boat team understand a set of a signals.
Here are some to try:

What You Mean	What You Do
Go faster	Jab your thumb up in the air.
Go slower	Jab your thumb down toward the water.
I'm not hurt	Always wave to the spotter after a wipeout.
I'm ok, pick me up	Bend your arm overhead, touch fingers in an "O".
I'm dropping the rope	Use your hand to cut across your neck.
I'm done, pick me up	Pat your head.

What Your Spotter Means	What Your Spotter Does
Wake ahead	Raise arm to the side and wave it up and down.
Stay straight behind the boat	Raise arm in front of body and wave it up and down.
We're turning around	Raise bent arm and circle with hand from the elbow.

YOUR WAKE MACHINE

Boat manufacturers now offer models specially designed for wakeboarding. Many feature built-in **ballast** systems or tanks that fill with water to add weight, which create a bigger wake. Some personal watercraft (PWC) tow wakeboarders, too.

Upgrading your family motorboat (with a parent's permission) takes some bucks and some time. Read the owner's manual. Talk to the boat dealer and the wakeboard parts supplier before you drill any holes into the fiberglass or wood.

WEIGHTY ISSUES

A small lip and a tidy curl tops off the best wake. Too much curl, and it's mushy without any pop. Too straight up, and it's rock-hard. Boats without ballast tanks might need help kicking out a ramp-ready wake.

Warning! Overweighting a boat will sink it. Check the owner's manual before you add ballast. Try inviting big friends. Well-stocked coolers work, too (until the end of the day). Wakeboard dealers also sell sacks that inflate with water. Be careful with buckets of concrete or bags of sand. They sink boats very quickly.

Add weight evenly to both sides, then front and back. Most open-bow boats need weight in the front for cruising anyway. Again, know how much extra weight your boat can handle.

HEIGHT HELPS

Wakeboarders often use a rope off of a tall **pylon** or tower centered on the boat. The extra rope height makes better jumps. Special racks also attach to the tower to stow boards and hold lights and stereo speakers.

A pylon or tower can cause the boat to tilt or slip sideways as the rider jumps. The driver must adjust for the action at the end of the rope.

The tower on this wakeboarding boat also has a storage rack for boards.

An experienced wakeboarder can show you how to hold a rope properly.

HOLD THE LINE

You won't go anywhere without a rope. Ask your wakeboard shop for wakeboarding rope. Don't use ski rope. You don't want any stretch or snap, called **recoil**.

Most ropes measure 75 feet (22.9 m), but newbies do well somewhere around 60 feet (18.3 m). Adding rope length will allow the rider to gain speed and airtime for bigger tricks. Advanced riders often use about 75 to 85 feet (22.9 to 25.9 m). Adjust the rope length for your boat and your skill level.

COOL COVERAGE

Competitions require helmets when the course includes ramps or other **obstacles**. But don't wear your bike helmet! Buy a special wakeboarding helmet that doesn't trap water. Also, don't board blind. If you usually wear glasses, talk to your parents and doctor about options. Prescription goggles, surgery, or disposable contacts might work for you.

Serious boarders also wear **neoprene** wetsuits when the water is cold. Wetsuits add warmth and they help you float. Lightweight spring suits or shorties keep you warm during cooler days. You might want a thick, full-length suit for early spring or late fall on northern lakes.

Each suit costs from $50 to $300 or more. Take care of it. Using it for a private potty is gross and stinky. Urine also ruins the neoprene. After every session, rinse your suit with fresh water and dry it, out of the sun.

RAD TIP

Cold and Cranky
Hypothermia starts with the shivers. It's time to head for shore. Warm up before you feel groggy or cranky. Hypothermia can kill. Sip warm water or tea.

UP, UP, UP

Every session should start with a pre-ride check of the boat and your gear. Are your PFD and bindings tight? Do your fins feel secure? Any wear or tangles in the rope? Tug on the knots at the boat and the handle.

Before you launch an air 360 (say: three-sixty), you must stand up on your wakeboard. Then you must stay up. Newbies often swallow a lot of water mastering these two steps.

chapter

THREE

READY, SET, RELAX

Use your PFD to help you bob in the water. Bend your knees with the bottom of the board facing the boat and your toes pointing straight up to the sky. Hold the handle with your knuckles on top. Make sure the rope drapes over your board. Put your arms out straight between your knees like you're reaching for your toes. Ready?

Yell to the driver for an easy, slow start. "Go, boat!" works. The rope straightens and you feel the tug. Focus on keeping your knees bent, holding your arms out straight and keeping your shoulders back. Stick out your chest, not your butt. Now relax.

PLANE TIMING

Newbies often try to muscle up. Let the boat do the work. At first, the pressure pushes your bent knees into your chest. Push back against the force. The board tip swings forward as it climbs up on top above the water. Stay crouched.

1. *Bob in the water with your knees bent and arms straight.*

When the board starts to plane, or skim the surface, you're ready to stand up. Again, the board must be on top of the surface or you biff. (You can't stand up too late, so try only when you're ready.)

As you stand, tuck the rope by your leading hip and bend your elbows. Holding the rope in front of your tummy is a fast ticket to a face-plant.

2. *Stay crouched until you are ready to try standing up.*

3. *Leaning back helps the board to plane, or skim, the surface.*

FOLLOW YOUR NOSE

You're up! Look at the boat or the horizon. Remember: the board goes where your nose goes. Look down and you go down.

Bend your arms slightly. Point your shoulders toward the boat and hold them back. If they roll forward, you'll tip too far ahead and face-plant.

Water must flow under the board. If you're plowing into the water instead of planing, lean slightly back on the tail to lift up the nose. Water rushes under and lifts you up. This also helps straighten the tail.

Your toes shouldn't point at the boat! Lightly lean on your heels to lift the front edge up, before it snags and knocks you for a painful digger.

RAD FACT

Where to Weight
Newbies stay up longer when they keep about 70 percent of their weight on the back foot. Advanced riders put equal weight on both feet.

Pressure on your heels or toes helps carve your turns.

27

If you live around snow, snowboarding is excellent for cross-training.

BODY CHECK

Nearly all major wakeboarders say that sticking to a workout routine notched up their performances. Surprise, surprise. Wakeboarding demands upper-body strength. Your legs put in overtime duty, too.

Work out at least three times every week. Lift weights. Do more push-ups than you can count. Build your quads, or thighs, and hamstrings with lunges and squats for solid landings and long sessions. Practice balancing. Close your eyes when you hop on one foot, then the other. Close your eyes when you stretch, too.

Stretch all of your muscles before and after a session. Hold each stretch for 30 seconds. You gain control, style, and balance. Strong, limber muscles also prevent injuries.

OUT OF THE WATER

Unfortunately, you cannot wakeboard 24 hours a day. A trampoline works great for trying new tricks. Skateboarding dials in control and balance. Mountain biking, in-line skating, and even old-fashioned running also help keep you in shape when you can't splash your board.

Do you live where winter brings snow? Try snowboarding. Snowboarders use the same muscles, movements, and some of the same tricks as wakeboarders. Also, check out some of the indoor roller boards, like Indo or Vew-Do, for carpet rides.

SAFETY CHECK

The driver, the spotter, and the rider must work as a team. Talk to the driver and spotter about the best route. Look for calm water in open stretches on rivers or lakes. Stay away from busy areas, sailboats, fishing boats, canoes and kayaks, and swimmers.

- Always wear a USCG-approved ski vest or lifejacket and a helmet.
- Always ride with a spotter in the boat.
- Check the weather forecast. Lightning and high waves can be dangerous.
- Slower is better than faster; stay at a comfortable speed.
- Stay behind the boat in traffic.
- No wake zones mean no wakes. Go slow.
- Never ride near docks, pilings, bridges, shore, or other boats.
- When you wipe out, always hold up your hand to help your driver and other boaters see you.
- Use common courtesy and common sense.

FREQUENT FLYER SECTION

Like surfers and other boarders, wakeboarders talk with a lot of **jargon**. A sick rider isn't hurling; he's throwing stylish moves. In wakeboarding, a roll means spinning rail over rail. A flip means turning tip over tail. Sometimes words fade out, too. Most kids don't say shredding (meaning excellent riding) anymore.

Wakeboarders who also ride in other board sports really watch their words. Surfers say frontside and backside to describe how they face the wave. Wakeboarders don't. They say toeside and heelside to explain how they edge up a wake. (Toeside means pressure on the edge under the toes. Figure out heelside.)

chapter
FOUR

MORE WORD WISDOM

Wakeboarders, like surfers, still use the words frontside and backside. But in wakeboarding, these terms describe which way a rider faces coming off a wake. So, the rider faces forward in a frontside 360. Backside and blindside both mean the rider faces backward coming off a wake.

Wakeboarding sites on the Internet often feature lists of more than 100 different tricks! Some moves come from snowboarding, surfing, skateboarding, and waterskiing. Other show-stoppers are pure wakeboarding moves. Riders invent more tricks every year, too. They give them names like Speed Ball for a double front flip (tail over tip, twice) and Tootsie Roll for a FS (frontside) roll (rail over rail) to blind (backside) 180 (half of a spin). Got it? That's why knowing the jargon helps.

SLIDERS, BOXES, RAMPS, OH MY!

Sliders, fun boxes, or ramps launched wakeboarding tricks to new heights. These obstacles float in the water, held in place with anchors. A slider, rail slide, or grind means the same thing: jumping out of the water onto a beam, then sliding along it for as long as possible before dropping back into the water.

Sliders often are made using two PVC pipes with space between them for the wakeboard fins or a wide, flat wooden plank.

If you handle a hammer well, build your own slider, box, or ramp. Find construction plans on the Internet and in magazines. Ask for permission before you sink money into your project. Many lake and river areas ban obstacles because smacking one the wrong way can be dangerous and deadly. Always wear your helmet. Don't try obstacles until you're up to it.

Ramps, sliders, and fun boxes add to the excitement at competitions.

RAD TIP

Built for Blast-off

Build your launch from the bottom up, making sure you use enough floats. Check that your design leaves room for the board's fins. Is the surface smooth? One screw sticking up could throw you off and into Pain City. Also, buy your materials. Do not steal the neighbor's PVC lawn chairs, no matter how ugly they are.

Use the wake for big air. Keep the rope low and your knees bent.

AAAAAIR!

Some wakeboarders scoot along behind their boats all day without sticking a single trick. They enjoy the ride as much as the champions flying off ramps. Wakeboarding is about fun. Ride at your skill level, ride safely, and ride stoked!

RADTRICK: SWITCHSTANCE START

Insanity Level: 1 of 10

Switchstance, revert, and fakie all mean riding the board opposite of your normal stance or backward. Reverts double your trick options and upgrade your skill level. Try switching your front foot when you're already up and riding behind the boat. Then try switching your front foot on a start-up, just after the board planes. Later, take it back one more step by pulling up from a revert position. Practice, practice, practice.

RADTRICK: WAKEJUMP

Insanity Level: 3 of 10

Before you get air off a wake, practice crossing it. Keep your knees bent and take it slow. Up, up, up, and over. For air, you need a bit more speed. Aim straight on. Carve your edge up the wake—don't flatten out until you're in the air. Tuck your knees toward your chest riding up the wake. Stay tight on the rope to hold the energy, or "load the line" for more spring. Use the rope like a springboard as you push off the lip with your legs. The rope stays low, near your hip. Look up and ahead. Spot your landing. Bent knees absorb the impact. Stomp it, and smile, smile, smile!

RADTRICK: SURFACE 180 AND SURFACE 360 / OLÉ
Insanity Level: 5 of 10

Start with the Surface 180 (say: one-eighty). Regular foot riders turn left; goofy foots turn right. Center your weight on the board. Press on your rear foot and let it lead the turn. Smoothly rotate so you face away from the boat, then adjust your weight to the front foot. Then turn from back to front again.

For the Surface 360, you turn in a full circle toward the left or right. Avoid tangling with the rope by passing the handle behind your lower back. Always keep one hand on it! Add some extra style with an Olé—the same move, but pass the handle while it's over your head. You'll have more control doing this one outside the wake.

RADTRICK: TAILBONE OR NOSEBONE GRAB
Insanity Level: 6 of 10

Skateboarders do Tailbones and Nosebones all the time. These moves look highly stylish as you fly off a wake. A *bone* means you stick out your leg—the front leg if it's a Nosebone and the rear leg if it's a Tailbone. Bend the opposite knee to help poke your leg out further. Now for real looks, add a *grab*—hold the board while you throw a move. Grab means grab. Sissy-slaps don't count. So a Nosebone with Tail Grab means that you hold the tail while you bone out your front leg. The longer and smoother you can do the trick, the sicker it is.

Notice how the rider grabs the tail—he doesn't just tap it.

With a lot of practice, you can work up to flips off the wake.

A RADTRICK: TANTRUM (AKA: TRIP-FLIP)

Insanity Level: 9 of 10

Plan on serious airtime for this move. Practice backflips on a trampoline for smoother **rotations**. A Tantrum is a backflip that uses the wake to trip you over (now you know why it's also known as a trip-flip). Edge hard for speed, cutting heelside as you reach the wake. Heelside edging gives you the kick for full end-over-end spin. Flatten off near the base of the wake so you lift up and not out. Let go of your back hand. Your back is to the wake as you throw your head back. Use your knees to push off and up, too. Practice tucking your knees up for faster spins. (After you master this, you can easily add a grab at this point in the move.) Spot your landing and land with your knees bent.

RAD TIP

Spinning Numbers

Wakeboarding takes a bit of math. In geometry, you learn that a full circle equals 360 degrees. So a full spin in a trick is a 360. A half spin is a 180. A spin-and-a-half? A 540. A double spin? 720. Just work the math. Sometimes riders just say one number, such as three, five, seven, nine, or ten. A 360 becomes a three. A 540 becomes a five. Go figure.

WAKESKATERS RIP ON THE WILD SIDE

Wakeboarders push for new challenges all the time. **Wakeskating** rips out there on the wild side. Instead of bindings, riders go barefoot or wear wakeskate shoes. Wakeskate shoes look like skateboarding shoes that let water drain out. Most importantly, wakeskaters stick to their wakeskates with sheer gravity (and luck).

A wakeskate looks like a fat skateboard deck with fins instead of wheels. The factory designs are smaller than wakeboards, topping out at 45 inches (114 cm). Serious wakeskaters use wakeskates with grip-tape decks, like skateboards. The rest use foam.

Wakeskaters also hop on boards they build at home, old wakeboards without bindings, or some other board that didn't come from a factory.

Better balance, tighter control, and some major guts separate wakeskaters from wakeboarders—especially in the trick department. Don't go there until you're ready. Really, really ready.

WATER WINNERS

Some sports disappear because the world rarely sees them. Wakeboarding burst onto the world scene and stayed there. Redmon, one of the first wakeboard designers, also formed the World Wakeboard Association in 1989. The WWA sets contest rules and sanctions events, including the U.S. Pro Tour, the Masters, X Games, Wakeboard U.S. Nationals, and the Wakeboard World Cup.

By 1992, Florida's World Sports & Marketing brought pro wakeboard events to crowds everywhere. ESPN and EXPN couldn't resist, and the world tuned into wakeboarding on cable. Soon, the Vans Triple Crown of Wakeboarding became a major contest. **Exhibitions**, like Boardstock on the Stockton Channel in California, attract huge crowds, too.

chapter

FIVE

Judges look for amplitude and smooth style.

WINNING WAYS

Judges watch for technical control and few wipeouts. They want to see huge **amplitude**, or height on airs, and a variety of moves. Creativity and smooth style also count in the total points that each rider receives. Judges also make sure every competitor uses the right gear, including non-stretch ropes, lifejackets or ski vests, and helmets.

Judges also send cry-babies home. Competitors and officials who throw tantrums (not the trip-flip type), swear, or act rude may face fines and lose participation privileges. Judges rule. Period. Don't talk back. Don't argue. Know the rules and follow them. Then stick your ride.

WORK, WORK, WORK

Sponsors choose a few wakeboarders to advertise their products or services. The pro wakeboarders earn money this way. It's not always easy money, though. You work for the sponsor and spend time signing autographs, talking to reporters, or riding demos when you would rather go hit the wakes.

Once you reach the advanced level, you can think about local sponsors. Ask your wakeboard shop or boat dealer. Some shops sponsor teams. Then you can hang out with other riders from your area and learn from them. Reps, or sales representatives, might sponsor you, too. The best of the best riders sign with factory sponsors like Liquid Force, Hyperlite, or Sea-Doo.

FRIDAY RIDES FINE ANY DAY OF THE WEEK

Many female wakeboarders take command of the wakes with fearless style. Dallas Friday ranks among the best in the world. She uses her strength and skills from her early days in gymnastics to boost her height and speed in aerial moves. After wakeboarding for only one year, she turned pro at age 13 and took the 2000 America's Cup in her rookie year! She helps with the national program to keep kids off drugs and she promotes the wakeboarding sport, too. Watch for Dallas in video games, movies, magazines, and, of course, ripping it up on the contest circuit.

FAN FOCUS

Name: Dallas Friday
Birthday: September 6, 1986
Home: Orlando, Florida
Height: 5'1" (1.6 m)
Weight: 115 pounds (52.2 kg)
Started wakeboarding: 1999
Turned Pro: 2000
Major sponsors: Fox Racing, O'Brien International, Malibu Boats, Bare Wetsuits, Mike's Place, Smith Sport Optics, and others

CAMPS TO CABLES

Ask riders like Dallas Friday for a tip to turn pro, and they will probably tell you two things: practice and have fun. If you're serious, attend a wakeboarding camp. You'll find all kinds of them on the Internet and in the magazines. Ask for references! Find out if the instructor really knows the sport or just wants fast cash. Find a buddy to tag along with you at camp. You bring back double the know-how.

Newbies and pros can also dial in new tricks at cable parks. The U.S. has three parks (so far), and cable parks have sprung up as far away as New Zealand. Instead of boats, wakeboarders ride off overhead cables. Each park offers different obstacles and all of them require helmets. The full-day rates range from $20 to $40.

TECHNOLOGICAL ADVANCES

Use technology to advance your skills, too. Ask your buddy, favorite member of the opposite sex, or a parent to videotape you while you ride. Small tweaks will dial in those moves.

Check out the Internet for instructional videos, too. Perfect for rainy days, videos let you study tricks frame by frame. Use slow motion and rewind to review the pro's moves. Watch the videos just for fun, too. Because FUN is what wakeboarding is really about!

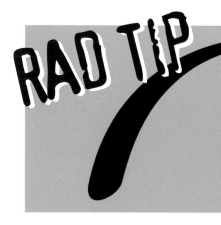

Scope the Park

Before you hook onto the cable in the park, watch the other riders. All of the U.S. cable parks use a cable design that makes it easier for goofy-footed riders. Scope the launch point and study how the riders edge, too.

FURTHER READING

Extreme Wakeboarding (Extreme Sports series) by Anne T. McKenna. Capstone Press, 2000.

Wakeboarding ...On The Edge by Jason Weber. Sports...On The Edge (publisher), 2000.

Wakeboarding!: Throw a Tantrum (The Extreme Sports Collection) by Chris Hayhurst. Rosen Publishing Group, 1999.

Wake Boarding Magazine

WEBSITES TO VISIT

www.mikesplace99.com

www.wakeboardingmag.com

www.watersportsindustry.com

www.thewwa.com

www.wakeworld.com

www.expn.com

www.wakeboarder.com

www.vans.comwww.OrlandoWatersports.com

www.wakewanaka.com

GLOSSARY

aerials (AIR ee ulz) — tricks or moves performed in the air

amplitude (AMP lih tood) — in wakeboarding, the height off of a ramp or wake

ballast (BAL est) — weight in a boat

biodegradable (bi oh dee GRAYD ah bul) — able to break down into natural materials; won't harm wildlife

compression molding (com PRESH un MOHL ding) — a way to make wakeboards and other products that use a form and pressure to create the shape

exhibitions (ex ih BIH shunz) — shows that focus on the performers' skills and talents, usually without awarding prizes or medals

jargon (JAR gun) — words that mean something special to a sport, hobby, or job

neoprene (NEE oh preen) — a lightweight, manufactured rubber used in wetsuits and other products

neutrally buoyant (NEW trah lee BOY unt) — in wakeboarding, a board that does not sink and does not bob up above the surface

newbies (NEW beez) — people new to a sport

obstacles (OB stah cuhlz) — in wakeboarding, the ramps, sliders, and boxes that riders use to launch tricks

perpendicular (pur pen DIK u lur) — positioned across something, like the top part of a "T"

personal flotation device (PUR suh nul FLO tay shun dee VICE (PFD) — a lifejacket or ski vest that helps your body float in water; always choose a PFD approved by the U.S. Coast Guard

pylon (PIE lon) — in wakeboarding, a pole-like device in a boat that holds the rider's rope high in the air to gain amplitude

recoil (ree COYL) — sharp, quick snap or kick backward

revert (ree VERT) — riding opposite of the normal stance or backward; revert, switchstance, and fakie all mean riding backward

rocker (RAH kur) — the wakeboard's upward curve at the tip and tail

rotations (roh TAY shunz) — spins, turns, or circles

wakeskating (WAYK SKAY ting) — a new sport that looks like skateboarding behind a boat; wakeskaters do not use bindings or attach themselves to the wakeskate like wakeboarders do

water-soluble (WAH tur SOHL u bul) — material that breaks down, or dissolves, in water

INDEX

ABOUT THE AUTHOR

Tracy Nelson Maurer specializes in nonfiction and business writing. Her most recently published children's books include the *Radsports I* series, also from Rourke Publishing LLC. She lives with her husband Mike and two children in Superior, Wisconsin.